All the Good
Devotions for the Season

All the Good:
A Wesleyan Way of Christmas

All the Good
978-1-7910-1797-2
978-1-7910-1798-9 eBook

All the Good: Leader Guide
978-1-7910-1800-9
978-1-7910-1801-6 eBook

All the Good: DVD
978-1-7910-1802-3

All the Good: Devotions for the Season
978-1-7910-1809-2
978-1-7910-1810-8 eBook

All the Good

A WESLEYAN WAY
of CHRISTMAS

Laceye Warner · Amy Valdez Barker
Jung Choi · Sangwoo Kim

·•· DEVOTIONS FOR THE SEASON ·•·

Abingdon Press | Nashville

All the Good: Devotions for the Season
A Wesleyan Way of Christmas

Library of Congress Control Number: 2021941864
978-1-7910-1809-2

21 22 23 24 25 26 27 28 29 30 — 10 9 8 7 6 5 4 3 2 1
MANUFACTURED IN THE UNITED STATES OF AMERICA

CONTENTS

WEEK 3: Caring for Others

WEEK 4: Sharing in God's Mission to the World

INTRODUCTION

Our Advent journey follows a path, one that leads us toward "all the good" of Christmas and Jesus Christ's birth. This Advent, that path follows John Wesley's guidance to practice "all the good" through the means of grace—or good works, practices of love of God and neighbor—in response to God's love and goodness to prepare for Jesus's coming as Emmanuel, God with us.

Means of grace are described in Scripture and continue as central practices of the Christian faith. While practicing means of grace is not unique to John Wesley, their practice is a prominent thread throughout Wesley's sermons and ministry in the early Methodist renewal movement. John Wesley wrote the sermon "Means of Grace" in 1739, relatively early in the movement. He later highlighted means of grace in his 1765 sermon "Scripture Way of Salvation," the most comprehensive account of Wesley's ministry and theology.

In "Scripture Way of Salvation," John Wesley begins with God's goodness and the essential doctrine of salvation. He describes salvation as available now—to all—as well as not yet, or after this life. For John Wesley, God's salvation is available to all through God's grace in Jesus Christ through the Holy Spirit. And God's grace is available through ordinary means described in Scripture and practiced in Christian discipleship. However, grace is not earned. God offers grace freely to any seeking God's love and forgiveness.

God invites all to receive God's grace. While God's grace and goodness may be found in and through all of God's creation, in Scripture we learn of ordinary means through which we may experience God's grace. Those means of grace include practices of piety or love of God through prayer, worship, singing, and silence. Means of grace also include practices of charity or mercy also described as love of neighbor through caring for the sick, hungry, and lost, and seeking justice for the oppressed.

John Wesley describes the means of grace in relationship to God's sanctifying grace in his sermon "Scripture Way of Salvation." In response to God's goodness and love for all in Jesus Christ, we are invited to practice God's means of grace in gratitude for God's love and goodness. By practicing the means of grace, in gratitude to God—not as a means to earn salvation—our relationship with God deepens. Through practicing the means of grace, God's holiness and fruits, God's goodness, grow in our lives, often sharing God's love with others.

The Scripture passages and devotions in this book provide an Advent path toward Christmas and "all the good" of God's grace in Jesus Christ. In the Scripture passages and devotions, we are reminded of the salvation narrative of God's goodness and grace in the world. We invite you to read each entry and reflect on how God is meeting us on the Advent path toward Christmas through God's means of grace.

Rev. Laceye Warner

WEEK 1
Preparing the Way
for God

> *A shoot shall come out from the stump of Jesse,*
>   *and a branch shall grow out of his roots.*
> *The spirit of the Lord shall rest on him,*
>   *the spirit of wisdom and understanding,*
>   *the spirit of counsel and might,*
>   *the spirit of knowledge and the fear of the Lord.*
> *His delight shall be in the fear of the Lord.*
>
>   *Isaiah 11:1-3*

My spouse and I were living in a parsonage, and we were the proud owners of a stump. A big one. It took up a large section of our backyard and belonged to what I imagine had been a glorious shade tree, offering comfort and beauty to residents and guests. The tree had been removed because the root system had begun to upset the stone path into our home, making footing treacherous and unsteady.

When the tree was removed, the contracted labor that had planned on returning a separate day to remove the stump suddenly disappeared. At the time, the congregation had adults well trained in disaster response and youth whose hands-on skills were exceptional. So these strengths were deployed on the stump.

For hours my spouse and I and watched student and adult alike rotate through with axes and shovels, hacking away at the stump. We even took our own turns, wanting to support the team in their work. In what seemed like a biblical way, the youth got weary...the young fell exhausted...and the adults grew frustrated. They were sweaty, sunburned, and dehydrated, and their well-intended plan to remove a stump had backfired. That stump stood in bold protest of their effort, a daily reminder not only of what was but also what was not: the pride of a team having accomplished a goal.

A shoot growing from a stump? How ridiculous! Just before this passage, God had doled out punishment to the people: "the tallest trees will be cut down, and the lofty will be brought low" (Isaiah 10:33). And yet the very same prophet then says there will be a shoot from a stump. A stump! The very thing that bears witness to what was and is no longer. It is from this place God brings forth new life. When we are exhausted. When we've been toiling, sometimes in vain, and when we feel as though we have nothing left.

When my team finally relented and brought in a stump grinder, we learned why our struggle was so intense. The deep roots had kept even the stump very deeply grounded. As we journey through Advent with the lens of Wesleyan theology, we remember the roots that keep us grounded, perhaps even upsetting some of the very established parts of our lives. We can, at the very same time, look for the signs of hope sprouting in unexpected places, even if those places seem cut down, dead, or otherwise abandoned.

We moved out of that parsonage almost a decade ago, but I was in the neighborhood recently. As I found myself absentmindedly driving past, I saw that the stump is still triumphantly established in the yard. It was different, however, because upon it was painted a heart. It might not have been a shoot sprouting up, but it was a powerful reminder to me of the ways that God's love and grace are being nurtured into the world through unexpected places. I hope that even when I feel cut down, I can be that tiny stalk of new life in a world that desperately needs it.

Rev. Anna Guillozet

DECEMBER 2

A highway shall be there,
and it shall be called the Holy Way;
the unclean shall not travel on it,
but it shall be for God's people;
no traveler, not even fools, shall go astray.
Isaiah 35:8

Among the many extraordinary things God does in our lives, God paves a highway for us. Not just any road, but a highway. Out of all places, in a desert! So why would God pave a highway in an abandoned place like a desert? For whom is this highway constructed, and where is God leading us to at the end of this highway?

In the beginning of this poem in Isaiah 35, we see that God is doing some significant work throughout this deserted place. God is changing the climate to turn a parched place into a land filled with plants and animals, full of diversity. God is restoring God's people even through their difficult challenges. However, the work of God does not stop here. The climax of this breathtaking work of God occurs when God paves a highway for those who were ousted to survive in this desert of scorching hostility.

Like many of our modern-day highways, ancient highways were often elevated from the ground. The paths were smooth and cleared of large stones. Those who once had to walk through the obstacles and the heat of life are now proudly uplifted, marching to return to God on this highway called "the Holy Way."

This powerful imagery of God's people, marching on their journey of holiness, reminds us of the peaceful marches of the civil rights movement organized by Dr. Martin Luther King Jr. God's work through Dr. King's ministry uplifted those who were walking through some of the most parched places of social inequality, paving the way for our continuing journey of restoring racial reconciliation and justice. His march was a bridge between the parched desert and the restored world of equality and diversity. His march became part of God's work in paving a highway to uplift those who were put out to walk through the fire of racism.

We are also called to walk on this highway called the Way of Holiness, to serve as a bridge between our own existing parched places and God's kingdom of restoration here on Earth. By doing so, we are also preparing the way for God to continue paving the highway, being part of the work of the Holy Spirit in uplifting inhabitants of the deserts in our world, as God transforms the climates of all of our parched hearts and minds.

Where are those parched places in your life and in our world where we desperately need to witness God's work of changing the climate? Who among us are still left behind in the parched places in our world? How does our journey on the Holy Way serve as a bridge between parched places in our world and God's kingdom of restoration? May our journey on the Holy Way serve as a powerful bridge of restoration. May our march be so transformative that we become part of providing a way for God, who paves a highway even in a desert.

Rev. Danielle B. Kim

DECEMBER 3

A voice cries out:
"In the wilderness prepare the way of the Lord,
make straight in the desert a highway for our God."
Isaiah 40:3

When the first child of Prince William and Kate Middleton (the future king and queen of England) was born, there was a guy ringing a bell and proclaiming the birth of their son outside Buckingham Palace, wearing clothes, a hat, and a wig that seemed more appropriate three hundred years ago. He didn't have an official role.

That he was not affiliated with the royal family or the British government was quite beside the point. An important person was coming onto the world stage, and he decided he bore the responsibility for letting everyone else know about it, whether anyone else approved or not.

When the president gives an address before Congress, the sergeant of arms of the House gets the honor of announcing, "Ladies and gentlemen, the president of the United States!" This is an official role, but almost no one knows who that individual is any other day of the year.

These modern examples suggest that there is something important about announcing the arrival of someone who is significant and plays a consequential role in the lives of everyone else, whether the role of announcer, or herald, is official or not.

Unlike at the outskirts of Buckingham Palace, and unlike in the chamber of the United States Congress, the prophet Isaiah announces the arrival of someone significant in places that are, well, not so significant.

The desert and the wilderness are other ways of saying "the middle of nowhere."

In Isaiah's time, the important places were gone. Babylon had sacked Jerusalem, destroyed the temple, and generally demonstrated that anything and anyone Israel considered important didn't matter one bit. A herald for the deity of a defeated nation? How silly!

Yet this is what Isaiah says. Contrary to the logic of all human societies, a messenger announces the arrival of a significant person who isn't considered remotely significant by everyone else.

In the Christian tradition, we see this passage echoing in the Gospels with John the Baptist. He wears animal skins and eats locusts and honey, just like the prophet Elijah. He's not at all subtle in recalling the heroes of Israel's past.

As obvious as John the Baptist is in what he's doing, he's only setting the stage for someone else to show up who is, likewise, not exactly what everyone else is expecting.

Jesus of Nazareth, the one who is God, who "moved into the neighborhood" (John 1:14 MSG), didn't meet anyone's expectations. The small number of Judeans who expected a messiah to show up and restore the kingdom of Israel were looking for a military leader. Jesus of Nazareth didn't fit that mold.

The way we human beings are inclined to read this passage from Isaiah, both the place and the person don't exactly work. The wilderness/the desert aren't a proper place for a significant person to show up. And a wandering preacher who isn't part of the religious system, a person who gets executed by an occupying empire, a guy who really doesn't amount to much in most people's eyes, does not match what we think the prophet is saying.

Yet that is what God is doing.

When we see something that defies our expectations of what God is up to, let's take a second look. Maybe, just maybe, someone is preparing the way for the Lord in such a way as to remind us that God is God, that we are not, and that's exactly what God intends.

Matthew L. Kelley

"Repent, for the kingdom of heaven has come near." This is the one of whom the prophet Isaiah spoke when he said,

> *"The voice of one crying out in the wilderness:*
> *'Prepare the way of the Lord,*
> *make his paths straight.'"*

Now John wore clothing of camel's hair with a leather belt around his waist, and his food was locusts and wild honey. Then the people of Jerusalem and all Judea were going out to him, and all the region along the Jordan, and they were baptized by him in the river Jordan, confessing their sins.

Matthew 3:2-6

Most of us do quite a lot of preparing for the Christmas holi days: shopping, wrapping, decorating, baking, planning, feasting… but not many of our preparations look like what Matthew's Gospel describes here. We might have special outfits picked out for the season, but not many will include camel's hair with leather belts, and most of us won't be preparing locusts and wild honey for ourselves or our guests.

John the Baptist looks quite strange in this passage, and yet his message is one that has lasted centuries, not least because of the tune of *Godspell's* "Prepare Ye the Way of the Lord." John invited all who had ears to hear—including us—to prepare in a different way than our usual shopping and decorating, saying that the way we get ready for Jesus is to repent, to turn from the life we've been living and set out on a new path, a straight road that goes right through the wilderness. He suggests that even if our lives have been pretty darned righteous to this point, we can't rely on that going forward: we have to keep making space for Jesus again and again, over and over, at Christmastime and throughout the year.

And maybe you're thinking that you don't have time for one more thing in a season that already feels overfull. But I bet we can all squeeze in some of John's important preparations as we get ready for this Christmas: we can spend time in self-reflection, asking God what we might leave behind after the holidays this year and what following Jesus more closely might look like. We can ask forgiveness for all the ways we've hurt or betrayed God, others, or the earth. We can simplify our lives and commit to new ways of living that are less focused on consumption and more on glorifying the Creator of all things. We can invite others to join us on this journey of faith. In fact, God is asking us to do *all* of these things as we get ready for the holiday, and *this* preparation is far more important than anything else we could do in the time between now and Christmas Eve.

One of the most encouraging parts about this passage is that it doesn't require us to get the "gift of the year" for someone else and wrap it expertly for the perfect Christmas surprise. It doesn't invite us to spend any money and doesn't chastise us if our social calendars aren't very full. In fact, if we're wandering in our own version of wilderness in this season, feeling lost, alone, sad, or afraid, John the Baptist is right there with us, promising that Jesus will be here soon. The gospel suggests that Jesus will meet us right where we are, no matter what we're going through, whether we've met Jesus here before or are waiting to meet him for the first time. All it asks is that we make some room—not under our trees, but in our hearts—to welcome him.

Rev. Elizabeth Ingram Schindler

"With the spirit and power of Elijah he will go before him, to turn the hearts of parents to their children, and the disobedient to the wisdom of the righteous, to make ready a people prepared for the Lord."

Luke 1:17

Over the past four years, I have been in the process of making a wooden nativity set for each of our four daughters. The first year I gave them the figures of Mary, Joseph, and Jesus. Then I added the animals, followed by shepherds. This year will be the magi. Such scenes are common in Advent and Christmas seasons. They remind us of the humanity of Jesus, and the quiet way he slipped into our world. These figures are often made out of materials that are fragile, such as porcelain, or fine wood that we don't want to scratch. We carry them gently. We tell children not to touch them. I have seen people approach a beautiful nativity and speak in hushed tones, as though they might wake the baby Jesus.

The baby in the manger, protected by adoring adults, is in contrast to the angel's description to Zechariah about his son, John the Baptist, our Advent reading from Luke 1:17. The angel predicts, "With the spirit and power of Elijah he will go before him, to turn the hearts of parents to their children, and the disobedient to the wisdom of the righteous, to make ready a people prepared for the Lord."

Elijah was the prophet who brought down the prophets of Baal and destroyed their altar so people would repent of their idolatry and return to the Lord. Elijah stood up to an unjust king who had lost his way. King Ahab and his wife, Jezebel, were so insulted by Elijah's words and so frustrated by his persistent actions that they plotted to have him killed. "Your son," the angel tells Zechariah, "will be like that." This child will also be a prophet who will turn many to the Lord. This verse does not come in a hushed tone, but in a shout. This text helps us understand that with the coming of Christ, God is not doing something meek and mild, but with the Spirit and power. John would point people to Jesus. He called them to repent of their sins and bless their neighbors who were in need. He would one day stand up to a king and lose his life for it. This proclamation does not put us in the Christmas mood, like figurines gently placed on a shelf. It rearranges the furniture. It reminds us not only of John's ministry and the way he turned people around, but also the life and ministry of Jesus. People would experience Jesus as many things: friend, physician, teacher, prophet, Messiah, and Christ. Both would shake up the world as they motivate us to actually live out the righteousness of God in our day-to-day lives.

This Advent, ask the Holy Spirit to shake up your world a bit to bring the goodness, righteousness, and joy of God where you live. What would happen if today, we would act in the power of the Holy Spirit, who leads us to change our world for good?

Rev. Tom Berlin

DECEMBER 6

As it is written in the prophet Isaiah,

"See, I am sending my messenger ahead of you,
who will prepare your way."

Mark 1:2

Have you ever had an experience when someone created a space for you and prepared a way for you? Throughout the world—and especially within the United States—there has been a growing awareness of the racial injustice and inequalities that are part of our communities. The prophet Isaiah spoke of the need for a new season and a restoration of what is broken—but before that restoration shall come, a path is laid by a messenger.

Who have been the messengers that have pointed the way to seeing what is not as it should be in the world? Sometimes these messengers have been actual people—people narrating brokenness and sharing images and stories in ways that cause thousands—if not millions—of people to see the truth. Other messengers have been groups, communities, and churches pointing to the need in the world and how we as Christians are called to respond. Still other voices have named the tension between the now and the not yet, pointing to what could be.

In this Advent season, practicing the means of grace can open our eyes to what is not as it should be in this world—and practicing the means of grace lays out the path to a life of accountability in righting these wrongs.

Advent is about a beginning, a looking forward, and an entry into a new liturgical year. In other words, Advent is about the now and the not yet. As you look ahead into the coming weeks, what are the means of grace that you are practicing? Are your individual works of piety (such as reading, reflection, prayer, and sharing your faith) bringing up common themes about a need in the world that is calling for your serving? Or perhaps your commitment to piety through the communal practice of accountability is drawing your spirit to God's directive in your life?

The means of grace are a way that God sends God's messenger ahead of you to prepare your way. Whether your path is beginning with awareness or grappling with actions and next steps, the messenger present in the Advent journey is clearing space for you. Even if you feel overwhelmed with the prophetic direction that God is pointing you in, this scripture reminds us that before each journey, there is One who makes a path for you.

For those who find connection in works of mercy, consider how your individual and communal practices take you on a journey to a more relational life. Our Wesleyan roots go far beyond cultivating a faith that simply connects the individual with God. Rather, practicing the means of grace through works of mercy ensures that we see our neighbors as real people and that all in the relationship are transformed.

Finally, just as the means of grace connect us to the body of believers, the messengers sent ahead of us remind us that our faith journey is not one of isolation. Even when God opens our eyes to what may feel like the overwhelming brokenness of the world, God reminds us that God sends God's messengers ahead of us to prepare the way for action. In this Advent season, may your eyes be opened to the path forward, and may your practices of the means of grace draw you closer to God and in deeper relationship with your neighbor.

Rev. April Casperson

Therefore the Lord himself will give you a sign. Look, the young woman is with child and shall bear a son and shall name him Immanuel.

Isaiah 7:14

Therefore, the Lord himself will give you a sign: The virgin will conceive and give birth to a son and will call him Immanuel.

Isaiah 7:14 (NIV)

Isaiah's prophetic vision is integral for Advent and Christmas for Christians, for the birth narratives of Jesus in two Gospels (Matthew and Luke) refer to this text by Isaiah. Christians believe that Jesus is the fulfillment of Isaiah's prophecy. The Gospel of Luke depicts a vital encounter between the angel Gabriel and Mary. Gabriel said to her, "Do not be afraid, Mary, for you have found favor with God. And now, you will conceive in your womb and bear a son, and you will name him Jesus. He will be great and will be called the Son of the Most High, and the Lord God will give to him the throne of his ancestor David. He will reign over the house of Jacob forever, and of his kingdom there will be no end" (Luke 1:30-33).

Prophecy oftentimes has some ambiguities and is mysterious and hard to fathom. To his people who went through series of tragedies with loss of their lands, homes, and family, and the exile into strange lands, Isaiah gave out this message of salvation and hope. Isaiah 7:14 does not say when the sign will be realized, whether it will be realized immediately or in the distant future. It is also complicated to tell whether the prophecy refers to the young woman (as the NRSV reads) or the virgin (as the NIV reads). The original Hebrew text uses almah (young woman). But its Greek translation, which was used by early Christians as the Scripture, uses parthenos (virgin). Despite these differences, the Gospel stories manifest God's powerful intervention with the broken world through the life of Mary (both a young woman and a virgin) and her faithful obedience to God.

The message is grounded in the hope of Immanuel (God with us), which reflects God's everlasting and faithful engagement with our world. God always invites people (especially the powerless) in God's grandiose engagement with the world, as we see in Mary's song (the Magnificat in Luke 1:46-55).

Prophecies and visions given by God illuminate other prophecies and visions so that their meanings are expanded and layered. Isaiah's prophecy and Gabriel's message to Mary illuminate each other, amplifying the good news of God's desire for the world. Mary's prophecy and Zechariah's prophecy (Luke 1:68-79) shine on each other. These prophecies are inextricably connected to many years of the Israelites' history, which emphasizes the loving relationship between God and human beings, and God's promise to deliver God's people from evil. These prophecies shed light on the lives of posterity. We believe Jesus's birth is the fulfillment of Isaiah's prophecy. Christmas and Advent are shrouded with mystery. Our own Christian journeys are also full of ambiguities and mysteries.

But we trust God's mysterious guidance; we trust that the Spirit of God, who inspires Isaiah, Mary, Zechariah, and countless people of God, is guiding us; we rejoice to live out the ever-presence of God through Jesus.

Thanks be to God.

Jung Choi

WEEK 2
Prayer

He was praying in a certain place, and after he had finished, one of his disciples said to him, "Lord, teach us to pray, as John taught his disciples." He said to them, "When you pray, say:

> *Father, hallowed be your name.*
> *Your kingdom come.*
> *Give us each day our daily bread.*
> *And forgive us our sins,*
> *for we ourselves forgive everyone indebted to us.*
> *And do not bring us to the time of trial."*
>
> *Luke 11:1-4*

"Lord, teach us to pray, as John taught his disciples," said one of Jesus's disciples. It was not a random request. Jesus had just finished praying, and the Gospel of Luke frequently shows how Jesus prayed (5:16; 6:12; 9:18, 28). The disciples had observed Jesus's habit of praying, and they wanted to learn from him.

It is intriguing that the disciples asked Jesus how to pray. As devout Jews, they were not strangers to prayer. In this story, however, no one assumes that prayer will happen naturally. Prayer is something we need to learn deliberately. John the Baptist taught his disciples how to pray, and Jesus's disciples wished to learn too. Here we can see that being disciples also means praying like their teacher. Praying is a distinctive mark of discipleship. Disciples pray as a community that shares their teacher's teaching on prayer.

In response to the request, Jesus taught them the Lord's Prayer, expecting his followers would be shaped in this practice. As disciples of Christ, we not only recite this prayer but also pray following Jesus's example. Other prayers in the Bible and liturgy also teach us how to pray. In our prayers for justice and mercy, prayers of lamentation and confession, and prayers for peace and love, we are nurtured and shaped. We become what we pray.

Jesus told us to be persistent in prayer. We can boldly ask in our prayers because we trust God as our parent. God will not grant our every whimsical wish. But Jesus assured us that in a loving relationship, God gives us life-giving gifts. Then, for what shall we keep asking, searching, and knocking? The gift of the Holy Spirit! Jesus said, "If you then, who are evil, know how to give good gifts to your children, how much more will the heavenly Father give the Holy Spirit to those who ask him!" (Luke 11:13). The readers of Luke–Acts get to learn how powerful and wonderful this gift is. They can see the work of the Holy Spirit in the life of Jesus—his birth (Luke 1:35), his baptism (3:22), his temptation (4:1), the beginning of his ministry (Luke 4:18)—and the life of the church: Pentecost (Acts 2) and the inclusion of Samaritans and Gentiles (Acts 8:17; 10:44–47). The Holy Spirit guides, nourishes, empowers, and transforms us. John Wesley saw the Holy Spirit as "the immediate cause of all holiness in us; enlightening our understandings, rectifying our wills and affections, renewing our natures, uniting our persons to Christ; assuring us of the adoption of sons, leading us in our actions; purifying and sanctifying our souls and bodies, to a full and eternal enjoyment of God."[1]

So, I am never tried of repeating this in my prayers: "Pour out your Spirit upon us!" Every night, when I pray for my children, I say, "Fill our hearts with your Spirit so that we can know and love you more and love our neighbors more." I know this prayer will be always answered as Jesus promised. In this Advent season, may we all receive the greatest gift of all: the presence of God's Spirit within, among, and around us. Come, Holy Spirit, come!

Rev. Sangwoo Kim

---

1. John Wesley, "Letter to a Roman Catholic," §8, in Wesley, *The Works of the Rev. John Wesley*, A.M., 5th ed. (London: John Mason, 1860), 10:82.

DECEMBER 9

And we are confident that he hears us whenever we ask for anything that pleases him. And since we know he hears us when we make our requests, we also know that he will give us what we ask for.

If you see a fellow believer sinning…you should pray, and God will give that person life.

1 John 5:14-16 (NLT)

Advent, which prepares us for the joyous celebration of Christ's birth, is a wonderful season of hope-filled longing and anticipation. In our homes, we decorate Christmas trees and place beautifully-wrapped presents beneath them—items chosen with great care for the purpose of bringing joy and delight to our loved ones. On Christmas morning, we eagerly unwrap our gifts without any trace of fear or dread because we know they are from those who love us and desire—even delight in—our good.

In a sense, this is an apt metaphor for prayer. God has loving gifts for each of us that we are invited to request and anticipate *with confidence*, trusting that God desires and delights in our ultimate good. This is essentially what 1 John 5:14-15 (NLT) tells us: "And we are confident that [God] hears us whenever we ask for anything that pleases him. And since we know he hears us when we make our requests, we also know that he will give us what we ask for." These words of the apostle John echo similar words spoken by Jesus on more than one occasion (Mark 11:22-24; John 14:13-14; 15:15; 16:24).

If we're honest, often this analogy breaks down for us when bad things happen or our prayers are not answered as we would like, because then we question whether God truly loves us and desires our good. But we find reassurance in the promise and power of the Incarnation. God, who is love (1 John 4:8), took on flesh and became a human being so that the love of the invisible God could be made visible to us in Jesus Christ. Jesus himself said, "Whoever has seen me has seen the Father" (John 14:9). Jesus was the perfect representation of divine love. He did not delight in the suffering of others but entered into their suffering with compassion and even was willing to suffer and die for the good of *all*.

Through Jesus we are able to experience the joy of a loving relationship with God and be transformed by God's perfect love, becoming more and more like Christ. This means that we can bring our requests boldly and confidently before the God who loves us so completely and selflessly, trusting that God is for us. Prayer is not begging God for what we want, as a child might plead for a Christmas present. Rather, it is learning to trust and delight in God's love for us so that ultimately our desires become God's desires (Psalm 37:4).

Of course, praying according to God's desires includes praying in love for all our brothers and sisters of faith: "If you see a fellow believer sinning... you should pray, and God will give that person life" (1 John 5:16 NLT). There is no better gift we can give to our brothers and sisters in Christ—at Advent or at any other time—than loving, life-giving prayer.

This Advent, may we pray with confidence to the One who loves us so much that God became one of us.

Sally D. Sharpe

DECEMBER 10

Let everything that breathes praise the LORD! Praise the LORD!"
Psalm 150:6

Have you ever forgotten to unmute yourself while in a virtual meeting or worship experience? Many churches have pivoted from in-person worship to virtual worship. The transition was easy for some but more difficult for others. One of the most common mistakes made by someone in virtual meetings is the failure to unmute. During one of our worship experiences, the soloist sang all six stanzas of "Amazing Grace" while muted. She was so focused on singing with her angelic voice that she didn't hear the pastor's numerous requests for her to unmute herself. Do you sometimes feel that your praise is muted by something? It may be a frustrating job, financial troubles, peer pressure, depression, or an addiction. Do you feel as though you have failed to click and unmute? Perhaps you sense that something in your life is just not working properly. But you must unmute and praise the Lord despite your circumstances.

As we prepare to celebrate the coming of Jesus Christ during the Advent season, we should be intentional about giving extravagant praise to the Lord, who became flesh to dwell among us. The Lord should be the object of our praise and the subject of our exaltation, because we are commanded to praise the Lord! Each of the five divisions of the Book of Psalms closes with a doxology. Psalm 150 is a doxology that not only closes the fifth and final division of the collected psalms but also closes the entire Book of Psalms. Psalm 150 provides a model for where, why, how, and when we should praise the Lord. We should praise the Lord in every place (v. 1), for every reason (v. 2), with every expression (vv. 3-5), and with every available breath (v. 6)! Psalm 150 is a song of praise designed to shine light on the majesty of the Lord. The psalmist uses the word *praise* thirteen times, and it can be translated "to shine," "to be boastful" and "to be made praiseworthy." Let the light of the Lord shine, so the world can be captivated by the Lord's majesty! Let the light of your hope, joy, peace, and love shine in your social networks! The psalmist entreats you to give the Lord unmuted praise everywhere you go and with everything you have!

Cary James Jr.

DECEMBER 11

The LORD is my shepherd, I shall not want
He makes me lie down in green pastures,
he leads me beside still waters,
he restores my soul.
He leads me in right paths
for his name's sake.

Psalm 23:1-3

It always happens. No matter how hard I try to plan or prepare for a restful Advent season, there's always a little bit of holiday hustle thrown into the mix. And with a crazy pandemic year under our belt, December 2020 was no exception. We were not one week into Advent when one of our campuses had to suspend in-room worship. With COVID cases on the extreme rise, we suddenly found ourselves pivoting yet again to a new online location, a new method of connection. This also meant that one of the most meaningful experiences of the Advent season, "Candle in the Night," had to change environments. I didn't want to change. Not again. Particularly not this event, when the entirety of the gathering was centered around helping people remember a beloved family member or friend who had passed in the previous year. It seemed like a sick joke, a double whammy. Folks are isolated and alone and the one gathering service you desperately need to attend—for closure, for comfort, for community—was moved online. It left many frustrated and wanting.

Our team did what we knew to do: we prayed and we pivoted. Prayed for God to make a way where there seemed to be no way. How could we be safe with the rise of COVID, how could this service and celebration be a source of hope for those who needed it the most? *Keep it simple*, was the Spirit's invitation we heard. Keep it simple and intimate. So, a handful of our team members—socially distanced and masked—began with prayer. And suddenly I heard those all-too-familiar words, *the Lord is my shepherd, I shall not want*. It's a passage people typically choose to be spoken or sung at their beloved's funeral, so it's fitting that these words might capture our hearts, our minds, and our thoughts during this season.

In moments where everything feels like hustle, as well as times when all around is loss, *the Lord is my shepherd*—guiding, directing, keeping our paths straight. When an entire pandemic season has felt like loss—the hundreds of thousands who've died as a result of this mysterious virus, a country in political turmoil, one black body after another, shooting after shooting, *even though I walk through the darkest valley, I fear no evil* (v. 4). But really, God, no fear?

Fear feels like our currency these days. Yet the psalmist David gifts us a different picture, a different path. In the middle of death and desolation, we find streams of living water, healing oil, a banquet—not in some distant, fairy-tale land, but right in the middle of the mess, in the very presence of our enemies, those men and women we want to call out, to reject, to other.

And so, we lit our online Candle in the Night. Through the simple gifts of our team—meaningful music, heartfelt prayers, a word of hope–suddenly I realized that, yes, even our deepest brokenness can heal. Our Facebook Live gathering reached more viewers than nearly any other service we offered throughout Advent. It wasn't polished, and it certainly wasn't perfect, but it was raw and real—a genuine digital space for healing.

Perhaps, my friend, in the middle of your holiday hustle, you can and will discover surprising spaces of peace and healing. Perhaps you will hear the invitation to embrace for yourself: *the Lord is my shepherd, I shall not want.*

Rev. Rachel L. Billups

...so that, with the eyes of your heart enlightened, you may know what is the hope to which he has called you, what are the riches of his glorious inheritance among the saints.

Ephesians 1:18

When I ask many Christians what they want to work on in their Christian life, a consistent response I get over and over again is prayer. Many of us have a sense that our lives should be ones of continuous prayer, but in reality, we experience a more sporadic or seasonal life of prayer. In the midst of our achieving and over-achieving society, the reality of our life of prayer over against our aspirations for our life of prayer might leave us feeling downcast. Thankfully, as the psalmist says, our God draws near to those who are brokenhearted.

Advent is not known for its simplicity in our broader culture. No, Advent is busy—there is very little that is still, quiet, or focused. Our hearts and minds can be all over the place, moving from highs to lows and back again as our hearts long for love, friendship, and family. We think of what we've gained and of what or who we have lost. Oh, how we hope during this season. In the midst of this range of thoughts and emotions, we may often say to ourselves, "O God!"

but sometimes we forget to finish the prayer. Yet God is always close to us.

I would invite you to a simplicity in prayer during this season that is sometimes not so simple. Consider joining with a church for its recitation of the Lord's Prayer. Taking those hours to be still for a few moments to pray those words and contemplate their meaning might be just what you need this season. Or maybe it's a prayer partner with whom to exchange daily prayer requests. Maybe you schedule a fifteen-minute slot on your otherwise busy daily calendar to sit and listen for God's voice. Whatever the mode or method—private, with others, aloud, or silently—take a simple step and adopt a simple discipline that may give life to your prayer life this season.

As we pray, our hope is that, as Ephesians 1:18 says, "the eyes of [our hearts]" will have enough light to see what is the hope of God's call, what is the richness of God's glorious inheritance among believers. We are hoping for just enough light to see things with a little more clarity during this season. We want to know the hope of God's call for us and all believers. Prayer is the time that centers and brings us beyond our brokenheartedness and our disorientation to a home—a home we find in God's presence. This home is a foretaste of things to come when all we will know is the richness of life in this home and the glory of the inheritance that we all have in God.

Rev. Justin Coleman

DECEMBER 13

But I say to you, Love your enemies and pray for those who persecute you.

Matthew 5:44

Just when we think we are comfortable and effective in our prayer lives, God steps in to lead us into deeper Kingdom expectations. It's a lifetime journey of discovery, and God provides extraordinary lessons along the way.

I learned my earliest prayer, "Now I Lay Me Down to Sleep," from my parents. This simple prayer both troubled and fascinated me. I struggled with the phrase, "If I should die before I wake," which fostered frequent discussion about death and the presence of a living soul in each of us. I recited this prayer every night with the wonder that as I closed my eyes, my last words of the day were spoken to an unseen God who would forever take care of me. Ironically, this bedtime prayer awakened me to the mystery of death and eternal life.

But as I approached my tween years, I began to experience feelings of unmet expectation. Something was missing in my childhood prayer, and I wondered if God really heard me at all. Then one day, I stumbled across a magazine article about prayer, written by the Rev. Billy Graham. On a whim, I wrote him a letter, asking how to pray so God would hear me. And astonishingly, he replied!

Graham responded with this advice: "Just talk to God like [God] is your friend, and take time to listen to what [God] has to say." This was a powerful revelation. Prayer is meant to be a two-way conversation. God's voice was that "something" I had been missing.

For years I happily walked this conversational path with God, settling into a confidence that my prayers were effective and mature. And that's when Jesus sent a message that rocked my world.

Following the destruction of the World Trade Center on September 11, 2001, a New York firefighter made a discovery in the rubble of the twin towers. It was an open King James Bible fused into a heart-shaped shard of metal. Amazingly, the two exposed pages were from Matthew 5—the Sermon on the Mount.

Although much is obscured by damage, you can see the beginning of Jesus's words from Matthew 5:44 on his law of love: "But I say to you, Love your enemies and pray for those who persecute you."

This turned my prayer life upside down…or better, right side up. I was used to comfortable prayer. To love and pray for those who wish to do us harm is hard. It's uncomfortable. It's not the way of our world. But Emmanuel—God with us—stepped into the heart-breaking rubble of our broken humanity to lead us into a better way. The Kingdom way.

Jennifer Wilder Morgan

"When you are praying, do not heap up empty phrases as the Gentiles do; for they think that they will be heard because of their many words. Do not be like them, for your Father knows what you need before you ask him."

Matthew 6:7-8

Jesus tells his followers to avoid piling up "empty phrases" when they pray.

Some students of the original Greek think the verb used, *battalogeó*, is an etymological immortalization of Battus, an ancient Greek bard known for his "tedious and wordy poems" (Thayer's Greek Lexicon).[1]

If this derivation is true, then I, as one whose ministry is a writing ministry, can't help feeling bad for Battus. To have one's name synonymous with "tedious and wordy" writing is awful enough. To have that association forever on Jesus's lips is a fate no wordsmith deserves, however artless their work may be!

Others think the word is an onomatopoeia—one that sounds like what it names—for stammering and stuttering. And so the King James reads "vain repetitions." But I'd hate to think Jesus is poking fun at people with speech impediments.

Why this warning against wordy, repetitive prayer?

Is Jesus prohibiting set, formal prayers recited time and again? Doubtful, considering how highly his own Jewish faith values prayers passed from generation to generation. The prayers we know by heart can reshape our hearts—or, more accurately, God can reshape our hearts through them, if we recite them attentively and thoughtfully rather than by rote. When I served as a pastor I found, as many pastors do, that people on their deathbeds who'd barely respond to anything would say Psalm 23 or the Lord's Prayer with me. Those texts had been on their lips and in their hearts for a lifetime, tools by which the Holy Spirit nurtured their spirits.

And while any words will do when we pray, I think trying to offer God the best words we can has its place as a spiritual discipline. To honor a retiring pastor, my childhood church published a book of the intercessory prayers he offered in public worship. He'd spend hours writing each Sunday's "pastoral prayer," polishing each phrase, stringing his sentences together like pearls on a necklace. When people asked him why, he'd tell them, "For the same reason I don't grab a bunch of weeds from the garden to show my wife I love her—I give her a beautiful bouquet."

God doesn't need and isn't impressed by "many words" when we pray. We can't badger God into noticing us by talking a blue streak. Flattery gets us nowhere with God, so we needn't try. God doesn't demand a minimum word count before hearing our prayers. God is already paying attention and is already aware of our needs.

Well-meaning Christian educators, myself included, sometimes tell children prayer is "talking to God." But lest we—like poor

Battus, perhaps—enjoy the sound of our own voices too much, Jesus invites us to find freedom praying with fewer words, and sometimes even with no words at all. The words we use to pray don't matter in and of themselves. They matter only to the extent they carve out space in our minds and hearts for an experience of God's grace and God's love.

Michael S. Poteet

---

1. *Thayer's Greek Lexicon*, Electronic Database (Biblesoft, 2002), "945. Battalogeó," Bible Hub, https://biblehub.com/greek/945.htm.

WEEK 3
Caring for Others

*Religion that is pure and undefiled before God, the Father, is this:
to care for orphans and widows in their distress, and to keep oneself
unstained by the world.*

James 1:27

Throughout the COVID-19 pandemic, nurses, respiratory therapists, doctors, and other medical professionals cared for others—many, many others—despite the risk to their own health and safety. Donning head-to-toe personal protective equipment (PPE) usually reserved for the likes of tuberculosis and measles, they rushed in to assess patients, administer medicines, adjust vent settings, hold hands, and facilitate phone calls with families, who weren't allowed to visit. Before returning to their own families, many of these care providers would change out of their scrubs in the garage and immediately shower for fear of exposing their families to this mysterious and vicious disease. Some even moved out of their homes for a period of time, all so they could care for these most vulnerable patients without becoming contaminated themselves.

Neither Jesus nor John Wesley was all that interested in keeping "clean." In fact, they were both criticized for reaching out to people in "dirty" positions and life situations. John Wesley left the pulpit behind and preached in open fields where crowds could gather.

He taught classes and organized bands in working-class neighborhoods and on the frontier. Jesus seemed to prefer the company of outcasts and those who were ceremonially unclean. In John 9, he even restored a man's sight using mud he made with his own spit. (Don't tell the CDC.) Jesus's ministry is proof that cleanliness is not next to godliness.

Still, both men had boundaries that enabled them to care deeply and give of themselves fully. For John, this meant keeping himself in pristine physical health so he could meet the demands of his intense daily schedule and practicing the means of grace to nurture his soul. Jesus regularly took time away from the crowds, engaged in prayer, shared meals with his closest friends, studied Scripture, and rested. These habits and boundaries served as their own sort of PPE, preventing contamination not from germs, but from compassion fatigue, bitterness, and moral exhaustion.

We hope now our health-care providers are getting some well-deserved rest and restoration. We hope they feel safer at work and at home, and they can consider their higher-level self-care needs, such as sabbath, restorative relationships, and time in Scripture. I'm sure they will still be getting their (gloved) hands dirty, as Jesus would encourage them to do, but perhaps the risk of contamination, literal and metaphorical, is lower, and there is space for them to consider what they need to do to take care of themselves in the midst of taking care of others.

What risks do you experience in caring for others? What can you do to proactively protect yourself from these exposures? What sort of spiritual and emotional PPE do you need to invest in?

Nancy Speas

*"I was hungry and you gave me food, I was thirsty and you gave me
something to drink, I was a stranger and you welcomed me, I was
naked and you gave me clothing, I was sick and you took care of me,
I was in prison and you visited me." Then the righteous will answer
him, "Lord, when was it that we saw you hungry and gave you food,
or thirsty and gave you something to drink? And when was it that
we saw you a stranger and welcomed you, or naked and gave you
clothing? And when was it that we saw you sick or in prison and
visited you?'" And the king will answer them, "'Truly I tell you,
just as you did it to one of the least of these who are members of my
family, you did it to me."*

Matthew 25:35-40

Having attended church since my feet barely dangled from the
edge of our family pew, I have heard countless evangelistic programs
captioned by the slogan "be the hands and feet of Jesus" or "you
are the only Jesus that some people will ever meet." In the famous
sheep and goats parable from Matthew 25, however, Christ flips that
messianic binary on its head, seating divinity squarely in the body
of the outcast, the unclothed, and the incarcerated. Jesus is not the
benevolent servant in this parable. Jesus is the immigrant and the
inmate, the stranger whose views set our teeth on edge, the neighbor
whose grief and hunger make us uncomfortable, and the sick friend

whose illness reminds us of our own mortality. As we reflect on the incarnation of Jesus, who chose to enter our world in naked frailty, experienced radical hunger and thirst, and suffered the incarceration and death of a criminal, we are challenged to love the strangers, the poor, and the prisoners who continue to embody the holy presence of the incarnate Christ.

Meeting the felt needs of others means attending to and believing those who tell us how they have suffered. It means inconveniencing ourselves regularly and unglamorously. During the years when my children were small, I remember longing for a project or a mission that would focus my energy on meaningful service. This parable from Matthew taught me that in the diurnal liturgy of motherhood, I continually clothed naked people, fed the hungry, offered bottles and sippy cups to the thirsty, cared for the sick, and welcomed these little strangers who upended every expectation I had about the limits of love and resources of my own heart. Every time I cleaned and bandaged a sidewalk-skinned knee, I unwittingly dressed the wounds of Christ. The disruption of their perpetual need had me tripping over the very threshold of heaven, precisely when I felt most anchored to the inconveniences of earth.

In my pastoral and professional life, projects, initiatives, and achievements threaten to eclipse the faces of hungry and thirsty people all around me. In my effort to accomplish personal goals, I sometimes ignore the shackled hearts and wounded words of the people serving alongside me. This parable reminds me of the high stakes attached to holy interruptions. The incarnate Christ still greets us in the face of the stranger. On my better days, the weight of my neighbor's need slows me down and compels my compassion. I find that, rather than being the "hands and feet of Jesus," I am moved by suffering that invokes the very wounds he carried there. Rather than casting myself as "the only Jesus someone may ever meet," I learn to see Christ in the eyes of every hungry stranger, and I feel deeply the sacred honor of sharing a meal. When we choose to embrace the grace of community with the weary, the hurting, and the oppressed, we daily honor the ever-present incarnation of Christ.

Amy Linnemann

You shall not make wrongful use of the name of the Lord your God,
for the Lord will not acquit anyone who misuses his name.

Exodus 20:7

I love tradition, and Advent is one of the seasons I enjoy the most. Marked by simple yet meaningful traditions, Advent always felt like a time of rejuvenation; a time when hope was plentiful and gave way to greater care for one another. It was a time of togetherness, a tender season whose themes of peace and joy, hope and love, always seemed to soften the harshness of winter in central New York.

During the COVID-19 pandemic, however, we all experienced Advent in a new way. The closeness of the season was placed in tension with health-stringent measures and church online. The safety guidelines may have felt like a litany from Exodus or Deuteronomy—some church signs cleverly said, "'Thou shalt wash thy hands' ~Hygenesis 20.19." These rules dictated our lives for over a year, and we had to adapt our Advent traditions—and our relationships—accordingly.

In Exodus 20, we're told that the Lord spoke to Moses and gave him the Decalogue, the Ten Commandments. But as a newly liberated people, why is it that one of the first communications from God was a list of rules? And perhaps even more strange, why are we focusing on these ancient rules in the third week of Advent? Well, if we take a closer look, we'll notice that at their core, the Ten Commandments are all about relationships—equitable and just relationships.

The Decalogue begins by orienting our relationship with the Divine, "You shall not make wrongful use of the name of the Lord your God" (Exodus 20:7). During this Advent season, may we be inspired by John Wesley's vision that Christian community ought to be a means of grace; let us reflect on how we might use the name of God as a means of grace in our relationships with others—especially with Black, indigenous, Latinx, LGBTQ+, disabled persons, people of color. After all, the first rule of Wesley's three simple rules seems to parallel the first commandment: "Do no harm."

The Decalogue continues with our own relationships to labor and with all those who labor: "But the seventh day is a sabbath to the Lord your God; you shall not do any work—you, your son or your daughter, your male or female slave, your livestock, or the alien resident in your towns" (v. 10). How might we care for those who labor this Advent season? How might we follow Wesley's second rule, "Do good," toward the overlooked and the underappreciated essential workers all around us?

As we find ourselves in this Advent season, enjoying the freedoms that come with quality health care, we can look back at Advent amid a pandemic, with its litany of rules, and see that at their core, those rules were also about relationships—about how we cared for one another. I invite you to look at the Ten Commandments again during this season of hope and reflect on how they could inform our relationships with others this year. How might our relationships with others be a means of grace for the world?

J. J. Warren

DECEMBER 18

When you reap your harvest in your field and forget a sheaf in the field, you shall not go back to get it; it shall be left for the alien, the orphan, and the widow, so that the Lord your God may bless you in all your undertakings.

Deuteronomy 24:19

Apple's iCalendar used to have a feature that would color dates yellow, orange, and red depending on how many appointments were scheduled on each day. There was a season in my life in which almost every day of the month would show up as red. When folks would extend an invitation for dinner, I'd respond with dates many weeks out. When someone walked into my office to chat with me, I'd watch the clock and end the conversation as quickly as possible so I could get back to work.

I was overbooked, overcommitted, and overextended. More important, I was not a good spouse, a good friend, or a good neighbor. I didn't have any margin in my life for other people.

On its surface, God's instruction about gleaning is about making a physical provision to care for the poor. Because leaving sheaves in the field for the orphans, widows, and foreigners was a requirement—like a tax rather than just a gentle suggestion for what to do with their leftovers—the Israelites knew they had to plan their crops carefully. They had to be sure that they would be able to live on less than their full harvest, since they would have to leave some of it behind.

I think the instruction is as much about caring for the souls of those with resources as well. The harvest was to be a time for blessing and sharing, not for greed. It offered them an opportunity to practice compassion and generosity, shaping their hearts more like that of Christ. And it offered an opportunity to practice trust in God's provision—that even if they left income-generating sheaves behind, God would still take care of them.

Very few of us today have fields of wheat or vineyards that we can strip bare, but we are proficient in stripping bare our other resources—especially our time. We commit to schedules that are sunup to sundown, and when God places opportunities in front of us to serve and love folks, we are often too busy or focused on our next thing to even see them.

The greatest gift that we can give others is the gift of our presence and our time. Like the Israelites, who planned to live on less than their full harvest, we need to be mindful of leaving some time and margin in our lives so that we can care for the folks around us.

Rev. Katie Montgomery Mears

Learn to do right; seek justice. Defend the oppressed. Take up the cause of the fatherless. Plead the case of the widow.

Isaiah 1:17 (NIV)

The memorable old FedEx ad opens on a corporate mailroom, where a woman is labeling packages. In walks a young man in a suit. Thinking he's there to help, the woman relates the simple instructions for preparing a FedEx shipment. "You don't understand," the man protests, sniffily. "I'm an MBA."

"Ohhh," the woman replies. "So I'll have to *show* you."

Unlike the haughty young executive, we can celebrate such words as good news: God cared enough to go beyond simply explaining how we are to live. God came to live among us and show us.

The law gave us the basic instructions: "Love God with all your being, and love your neighbor, created, like you, in God's image."

The prophets added practical applications: Practice doing what is right. Seek justice, always. Stand up for the oppressed (and correct the oppressors). Protect those who have no strong protectors. Be a champion for those who have no advocate. Help the helpless. Reach out to the outcast. Love kindness. Extend mercy. Walk humbly.

The instructions were misunderstood or ignored. So, in the divine person of Jesus, God came to show us.

Jesus's acts continuously demonstrated how to live in God's kingdom. He showed what mercy and compassion look like. He took up the cause of a widow whose only son (and means of support) had died, restoring the young man to life. He restored outcast lepers and blind beggars to health—simultaneously restoring them to their community. When a notoriously sinful woman crashed a dinner party held in Jesus's honor, desperate for what she believed Jesus had the power to bestow, he championed this person who had no other advocate, and showed his startled host how to practice radical, restorative forgiveness.

All these gracious acts were demonstrations of God's justice—that is, the condition that prevails when human beings are treated with the love and dignity that are their birthright as children of the Creator.

It's little wonder that Isaiah 1:17 has become a favorite text for the Black Lives Matter movement. In declaring that he came to bring good news to the poor and release to those who are bound, Jesus sent an electrifying message. In God's kingdom, now here, the poor at last are honored members of the beloved community. Poor lives matter. Outcast lives matter. Oppressed lives matter. Imprisoned lives matter. And when we seek God's justice for lives that have not mattered enough to our society, we also claim the power to become the fully realized human beings whom God always meant for us to be. It is why John's Gospel could say that what came into the world through the Incarnation was light, and that light was *life* for all humankind. Jesus didn't just deliver instructions. The Teacher came and showed us, lighting the way.

Randy Horick

No one has greater love than this, to lay down one's life for one's friends.

John 15:13

In John 15, Jesus begins with an image that permeated the Old Testament Scriptures and finds its place in the Synoptic Gospels. True to Jesus's style, he used visuals that surrounded his readers in their everyday lives; he spoke in a language they could understand.

This vine/branch image and its use of the word *abide* (v. 4) is meant to expose an abiding thread in the Book of John. If we pay close attention to the writers of Scripture, we see how they pull certain threads taut throughout their work, weaving a beautiful tapestry that connects one piece of their book to another.

Here, *abide* has a cognate, a noun that is used in John 14:2. The many dwelling places of the Father's house are abiding places. Both images are supposed to alert our minds to the abiding love of Jesus. As we make a home in Christ, we learn to love like Christ. As we ground ourselves in the stem of life, we branch out and flourish with fruit.

It is this context that takes us to Jesus's Last Supper reminder "to love one another as I have loved you" (John 15:12). Jesus then adds: "No one has greater love than this, to lay down one's life for one's friends" (v. 13).

Scholars say that when Jesus appeared to Peter by the Sea of Tiberius in John 21, he alluded to this line from John 15:13. At the Last Supper, Peter was so willing to lay down his life for Jesus, but when the time came, he abandoned his pledge.

As Jesus reinstates Peter, he gives him a second chance. Jesus explains how Peter will be martyred, and then issues the same invitation with which he first called Peter: "Follow me." As we know, Peter goes on to fulfill his declaration of greater love. This time, he offered more than his lip service to Jesus; he pledged and gave up his entire life.

For most of us, laying down our lives for our friends will not result in literal death. And so we must consider what it does mean.

In my own life, I have witnessed this laying down of self through care. I picture my own mother, a single parent with three children under five years old, working full-time to provide for us. I picture a man in my church caring for his ill wife, washing her hair, changing her clothes, carrying her up flights of stairs.

Yet, I have noticed that what I call sacrifice, these people in my life simply call love. It isn't a burden, but an extension of the love that dwells within them.

Perhaps then, to lay down one's life for one's friends is to give up slices of Christ's love that grow within us. Perhaps it is to part ways with the capacity for compassion that inhabits us at our core.

As we abide in Christ, laying down our life feels less like sacrifice; it is simply love.

Rev. Sam McGlothlin

DECEMBER 21

The commandment we have from him is this: those who love God must love their brothers and sisters also.

1 John 4:21

For John Wesley the wonder of Christianity—especially Advent and Christmas—is God's unconditional love for all. For Wesley the marks of Methodism were not particular technical distinctions of beliefs that set Methodists apart from other Christians. Wesley was also not concerned about building a movement to compete with other churches. Rather, John Wesley was called to share God's love, which he had received, with anyone willing to listen.

The theme of love of God and neighbor is a persistent thread throughout the Bible, beginning in the Old Testament. The refrain to care for widows, orphans, and strangers echoes throughout the Bible as a response to God's love: from Israel's time as strangers in a strange land and later as a nation, through the Advent and Christmas narratives of Jesus's birth, and later in his incarnational ministry as God with us.

The persistent biblical theme of loving God and neighbor captured in the Advent and Christmas narratives provides the frame through which we understand our Christian faith. Similar to the essentials of food, water, and exercise that sustain human life, practices of loving God and neighbor provide the essentials for flourishing lives of faith within Christian community.

At times Christians can be deluded—even manipulated—into claiming identity through accomplishments and power defined by worldly standards. While such identities are actually unsustainable, many attempt this impossible task. Identity not rooted in God leads to an insatiable thirst for new and better techniques, in pursuit of success masquerading as effectiveness, resulting in perpetual fatigue, or worse, loss of purpose . . . and even faith.

Baptism defines our identity as unique beloved children of God created in God's image. As beloved children of God, we are incorporated into the body of Christ. Of all our identities—friend, parent, child, sibling, professional, hobbyist—our identity as beloved children of God will persist through this life and the next. As beloved children of God, we are called to share God's love, which we have received unconditionally, with all of creation.

Whether we are new or seasoned Christians, it is our identity as beloved children of God, our relationship to God, and our calling to love all of God's creation that gives us identity and purpose in this life and beyond.

In his "The Character of a Methodist," John Wesley answers the questions "Who is a Methodist?" and "What is the mark?"

His response? "A Methodist is one who has the love of God shed abroad in [one's] heart."[1]

In this season of Advent, as we await the birth of the Christ child, Emmanuel, God with us, may we remember God's love for us. And may God's love invite us to respond by sharing God's love with others.

Rev. Laceye Warner

---

1. John Wesley, "The Character of a Methodist," 2.5, *The Bicentennial Edition of the Works of John Wesley* (Nashville: Abingdon Press, 1976), 9:5.

WEEK 4
Sharing in God's Mission to the World

The LORD said to Abram, "Leave your land, your family, and your father's household for the land that I will show you. I will make of you a great nation and will bless you. I will make your name respected, and you will be a blessing.

> *I will bless those who bless you,*
> *those who curse you I will curse;*
> *all the families of the earth*
> *will be blessed because of you."*

Genesis 12:1-3 (CEB)

"Jorge, did you know that there are children living on the streets of Fort Lauderdale?" Fred asked early one morning at our men's small group. I took a sip from my coffee, then retorted, "Yes, Fred. It's sadly true. So, why don't you do something about it?" From that simple conversation, a God-sized mission was placed in Fred's soul. Twenty-five years later, Hope South Florida is the largest provider for families experiencing homelessness in Broward County, sharing more than two thousand meals a week, offering housing for more than two hundred families, with a $5 million budget and thirty employees. And it all began in the conference room of our church.

Like Abram and Sarai, Fred, an overly entertained, bored veterinarian, became an everyday missionary for Jesus. When God tapped

Abram on the shoulder millennia ago and told him to start walking and that God would tell him when to stop, God also promised him that God would bless him to be a blessing. God's blessing never was or is an end in itself. We are blessed to bless others. The apostle Paul, after beautifully affirming that we are saved by faith alone apart from works (Ephesians 2:8-9), adds this spiritual truth in verse 10: "For we are God's handiwork, created in Christ Jesus to do good works, which God prepared in advance for us to do" (NIV). We are not saved by works but indeed we are saved for works. This is living a "blessed to be a blessing" life. This is being an everyday missionary. This is displaying God's unique handiwork through you.

Years ago, I heard someone say, "The heartbeat of the city is where the pain is." This Advent season, as you make your way to Christmas parties, church activities, and shopping sprees, ask God to give you "eyes to see" the pain in your community. To what pain-filled place might God invite you to go and be "Jesus with skin on"? Abram, Sarai, and Fred had no idea what that prompting from God would lead to. You won't either, but I can promise you this: it can change your life and the life of others as you live the "blessed to be a blessing" life.

God, I am open and available to your tap on my shoulder, inviting me to start walking. I'll stop when you tell me to stop, as Sarai and Abram did. As you did for Fred, open my eyes to the pain in my city. Let my heart break for what breaks yours. I pray in the name of the One born into our broken and pain-filled world, Jesus. Amen.

Jorge Acevedo

DECEMBER 23

"Now therefore, if you obey my voice and keep my covenant, you shall be my treasured possession out of all the peoples. Indeed, the whole earth is mine, but you shall be for me a priestly kingdom and a holy nation. These are the words that you shall speak to the Israelites."

Exodus 19:5-6

When I consider the material possessions in my home that are the most treasured, it would probably surprise many that they are, without a doubt, some of the most unassuming. There's the old wooden rocking chair bought by my grandparents in 1910 at the birth of their first child. It rocked seven children to sleep at night, was the centerpiece of family hymn singing on their front porch, served as the official gathering place for hundreds of family Christmas photos, and continues to rock a sixth generation of babies as their weary parents and grandparents cradle them in their arms during midnight feedings.

Next is my mom's simple pottery serving bowl. It faithfully held the vegetable du jour at our dinner table each night, and generations of gathered family members were nourished by its generous offerings at every holiday meal.

The third is a modest little string of pearls purchased in 1952 by a twenty-one-year-old young man who'd scrimped and saved to purchase the finest gift he could afford to honor his sweet bride-to-be. That bride offered those pearls to me at my wedding to her son, and they have since been gifted to our daughter, who never had the chance to meet the extraordinary man who had worked so hard to offer a token of his love to the one he loved most.

These possessions are treasured, not for their meager monetary value, but for the priceless reminder of unconditional love and acceptance, marked by the steady drum of indefatigable faithfulness, passed from generation to generation.

Something set apart for God's purposes is deemed *holy*. Exodus recounts the story of God's mighty and disruptive coming into the midst of a people beloved by God since before their conception. God covenanted with their ancestor Abraham that if he obeyed God's voice, he and his wife, Sarah, would give birth to a great nation. Their purpose? To live in such a way that all nations would come to see the depth of God's love and faithfulness through them. Generations later, the Israelites stand at Mount Sinai, freed from slavery in Egypt by the God who treasures them, and listen to a new iteration of the covenant. Keep the covenant, by loving God and their neighbor, as set forth in the Ten Commandments, and they will be God's treasured possession, a priestly kingdom, and a *holy* nation.

Each Christmas season, we are reminded of the powerful and disruptive coming of God in the flesh of the Christ child to claim all the world as his treasured possession. We become that treasured possession through the gift of God's treasured Son, who exhibited the deep love and faithfulness of God *toward* us by giving up his life *for* us. We live into our purpose as Christ's treasured and holy possession when we continue his unchanging mission: to live in such a way, by imitating his life, that all people will come to see and know the depth of God's eternal love and faithfulness through us by the power of his Spirit. Just as he fed the hungry, brought healing to the sick, included and accepted those rejected by society, and shared in word and deed the abundance of God's love, so must we.

I think the original owners of my treasures would be surprised to know not only that their simple possessions still existed but also the lasting impact of the love they shared through those possessions on future generations.

You are God's treasured possession. You may never see how the way in which you share the gift of Christ's love and faithfulness today impacts generations to come, but it will. May you receive the treasure of Christmas this season and share it generously always.

Rev. Susan Robb

And he came to her and said, "Greetings, favored one! The Lord is with you." But she was much perplexed by his words and pondered what sort of greeting this might be. The angel said to her, "Do not be afraid, Mary, for you have found favor with God. And now, you will conceive in your womb and bear a son, and you will name him Jesus.

Luke 1:28-31

Mary was confused. Who wouldn't be? The possibility of having a baby seemed downright impossible! With her, we ask, "How can this be?"

Try explaining the Incarnation gynecologically and your brain will get tangled up like that old string of lights you pulled from a box to hang on your tree. What if the key to the story is not what it says about Mary, but what it says about Jesus?

To declare that "the Word became flesh" through Mary is to believe that in Jesus we see as much of God as could be squeezed into human flesh (John 1:14). It's why Charles Wesley sang, "Our God contracted to a span,/Incomprehensibly made man." While it's impossible to say that Jesus is like God, it's now possible to declare that God is like Jesus. The impossible has become possible through Mary.

It may, however, be easier to accept a virgin birth than to believe that the Word continues to become flesh through people like Mary; to believe that the Kingdom vision Mary celebrates in the Magnificat (Luke 2:46-55) becomes a reality in this world through ordinary people like us!

How can *that* be? "The Holy Spirit will come upon you, and the power of the Most High will overshadow you.... For nothing will be impossible with God" (Luke 1:35, 37). By the power of the Holy Spirit, nothing that is consistent with the kingdom of God revealed in Jesus is impossible for God. Nothing that looks like God's love made flesh in Jesus being made flesh in us is impossible for God!

The impossible becomes possible when we live into Mary's prayer, "I [am] the servant of the Lord; let it be with me according to your word" (v. 38).

In her Christmas letter to friends and family, a woman whose husband had died unexpectedly that year wondered, "How is it possible that in the midst of heartache I found God in the power to keep going?" She concluded, "Christmas is the promise that God can be trusted to meet all our needs, sometimes in ways we would never think possible. Without my husband, Christmas will be very painful. But without Christmas my life would be impossible."

How can this be? Through people like us, God still gives birth to things that by the world's standards are impossible.

James A. Harnish

Now the birth of Jesus the Messiah took place in this way. When his mother Mary had been engaged to Joseph, but before they lived together, she was found to be with child from the Holy Spirit. Her husband Joseph, being a righteous man and unwilling to expose her to public disgrace, planned to dismiss her quietly. But just when he had resolved to do this, an angel of the Lord appeared to him in a dream and said, "Joseph, son of David, do not be afraid to take Mary as your wife, for the child conceived in her is from the Holy Spirit. She will bear a son, and you are to name him Jesus, for he will save his people from their sins."

Matthew 1:18-21

Christmas Day is the advent of healing. I love the Christmas story because deep down it's the story of a healed marriage through Jesus's presence. Perhaps this Christmas story can speak to some of the relationships you need to invite Jesus in and heal.

Let's set the scene. Joseph was married to Mary. They were legally married but not living together yet. Joseph was hard at work preparing a house for him and his new bride to live in. While working hard to provide for her, Mary turns up pregnant.

How would you feel if your spouse became pregnant and claimed God did it?

Can you imagine the crying Joseph did, or maybe the anger that he felt? He's been publicly shamed. He's about to go through a divorce, which would have been customary in his day given his situation. He hasn't even consummated his marriage yet and it's now over. Joseph is mourning the brokenness of his failed marriage.

Yet when Jesus shows up in a situation, he brings healing in his wake. When Jesus is involved, he takes broken things and makes them better. Jesus redeems the pain and hurts we suffer in all areas of our relationships. While Mary herself didn't technically do anything to Joseph, there is a lot for them to heal through together.

Here is the thing about being relationally broken. When things fall apart, we are limited in our perspective. When life is in pieces, it's nearly impossible to see the bigger picture. This is when faith has to kick in. When life and relationships fall apart, have faith that the God who loves you, who came to save you, can put the pieces back together again. They might never fit back in the same way; still, God makes good things out of failures and broken dreams. Don't give up yet. Don't throw in the towel.

You may feel like Humpty Dumpty, broken to pieces. And while all the king's horses and all the king's men can't put you back together again, the King can. Christmas is the celebration that the King has arrived. His advent is the source of healing and grace in even the most damaged relationships.

Joseph thought his life was over, but God had another plan, a bigger plan, one that could only be told through the bumps and bruises along the way. We tend to think of pain, hurt, and brokenness only in a negative way. While it is miserable when you're in the middle of it, if Jesus is involved, grace and healing are not far behind. God redeems the brokenness. Don't deny God that opportunity this Christmas Day.

So what do you do with the relationships that need healing now? Stay open to what God wants to do. Ask for forgiveness to the parts you played. Give forgiveness to the parts the other played. Be open to reconciliation. Come to the manger and meet this Child who comes to save, and pray that the other person comes to the manger too. If you're both in the presence of Jesus, God's got the option to do some major healing in you. Don't miss the opportunity to let Jesus bring healing and restoration to you this Christmas.

Rev. David Dorn II

> "Then I heard the Lord's voice saying, 'Whom should I send, and who will go for us?'
>
> I said, 'I'm here; send me.'"
>
> *Isaiah 6:8 CEB*

I've never been a great language-learner, although I've tried my hand at several: French, Spanish, Latin, and biblical Greek. You can ask my teachers: whether from lack of skill or lack of discipline (or probably both), I wasn't a star language student. But I love the idea of languages. I love that my bilingual friends often dream in more than one language. I love that some languages have words for things that English does not. *Lagom*, in Swedish, means "just the right amount" of something, and also refers to having a balanced life. *Gigil*, in Tagalog, means the overwhelming of your self-control—like when the cuteness of something makes you want to hug it so much that you can't control yourself. I love that these concepts, even if I can't speak the languages, expand how I think about things.

When the prophet Isaiah is called to that ministry, initially he protests, saying, "but I am a man of impure lips." So an angel comes with a burning coal and purifies Isaiah's lips. A teacher once said that before this sign-act, Isaiah spoke in prose, the language of ordinary folks.[1] Now, Isaiah is able to speak in poetry, the language of the prophets. So when God asks, "Who will go for us?" Isaiah now feels equipped to say, "I'm here; send me." Isaiah now speaks the language of God.

All of us, whether we're good language students or not, have this same experience when we are called to be a part of God's work in the world. All of us, when we listen to the voice of the Holy Spirit, begin to hear and understand in new ways. The world speaks of the great skills of talented people. But we understand that everything is done by God's power, not our own, and that all our skills are just gifts from God. The world speaks of individual accomplishment and seeking good just for ourselves. But in God's language, everything is done for the good of all creation. The world speaks of resources being limited. God's language reminds us of the great abundance that is enough for everyone. It is a new way of thinking, speaking, and acting in the world. It is the language of transformation—when we begin to think and live in that language, things around us change.

The anticipation of the coming of Jesus—both into the manger and into our world again—is a reminder of this language of transformation, which is in fact our mother tongue. As you look for this new birth, how are you using God's language, and how does this new language change you and change the world around you?

Rev. Monica Beacham

---

1. Robert Alter, *The Hebrew Bible: A Translation with Commentary: Prophets* (New York: W. W. Norton, 2018), 642.

DECEMBER 27

Now the eleven disciples went to Galilee, to the mountain to which Jesus had directed them. When they saw him, they worshiped him; but some doubted. And Jesus came and said to them, "All authority in heaven and on earth has been given to me. Go therefore and make disciples of all nations, baptizing them in the name of the Father and of the Son and of the Holy Spirit, and teaching them to obey everything that I have commanded you. And remember, I am with you always, to the end of the age."

Matthew 28:16-20

Perhaps you think it is strange to be reflecting on Jesus's final resurrection appearance during the Advent and Christmas season. Maybe it is. Yet, it offers an important word for now and throughout the upcoming new year.

Call to mind a time when you sensed a calling from God to do something unfathomable, something you didn't think you could do. It could have been a calling to do something big or something out of your comfort zone. Maybe your history, life experience, knowledge base, skill set, financial or emotional resources, and the conditions around you convinced you that what God was calling *you* to do didn't make sense. You said to yourself (and maybe to God), "Nah, I am not qualified for *that* calling."

If you haven't had that experience, and you are trying to follow Jesus and live out the call to love God and love neighbor—just wait; you will.

One such moment for me was when I was discerning whether to become a minister. I was working at a church but was feeling like a fraud. Growing up, I wasn't a regular participant in a faith community. I didn't understand the church lingo or the culture and had no youth group memories from which to draw. I had a checkered past, had no formal Bible training, was in recovery from drugs and alcohol, and only recently had devoted my life to Jesus Christ. Not only was I way outside my comfort zone working at a church, I now was embarking on the long process of ordination (which included seminary while raising two young kids).

As this was unfolding, I was approached and eventually offered a job to leave the church and lead a not-for-profit agency. I was much more qualified for it than for becoming a minister. Everything in my head said, "Take it and run." I was filled with doubt about being a spiritual leader. If I continued, I would be expected to lead people to a deeper relationship with Christ and the church. Preaching terrified me. I knew with certainty that I wasn't qualified to do *that*. During this unsettling and scary time, I met with a spiritual mentor, who reminded me that "God doesn't call the qualified; God qualifies the called."

The disciples, minus Judas Iscariot, heard that message on that unnamed mountain in Galilee. Yet, going back to their previous lives would have been easier. Verse 17 of today's passage says they worshiped, but some doubted. Doubt was understandable, since by every measure, they were the definition of unqualified. Jesus's last words to them were a monstrous, audacious calling that included instructions and a promise. They were to go out to people unlike them, make them disciples, and teach them to love God, others, and enemies. His promise? That he'd be with them always.

You are called to make God's love real in this world. Your experience, skill set, history, and conditions will suggest otherwise. You will doubt. Do it anyway. Doubt is part of the journey. Jesus Christ will never leave you.

God's promise is what Advent is all about. Maybe reading this text during this season isn't strange after all.

Rev. Justin LaRosa

"He has told you, O mortal, what is good;
and what does the LORD require of you
but to do justice, and to love kindness,
and to walk humbly with your God?"
Micah 6:8

As Christmas day loomed, we may have felt a mix of happy anticipation and panic. For many, there was a rush to finalize menus, plans for gatherings, or purchasing just the right gifts. I am generally in awe of those who seem to get it all done without a frenzy.

But, regardless of how we manage the traditional, cultural tasks connected with the last week of Advent, we all receive a helpful reminder in Micah 6:

"With what shall I come before the LORD
and bow myself before God on high?
Shall I come before him with burnt offerings,
with calves a year old?
Will the LORD be pleased with thousands of rams,
with ten thousands of rivers of oil?" (vv. 6-7a)

The question is, What is on God's wish list? What gifts or gatherings or nourishment does God desire?

And the prophet makes it plain:

"[God] has told you, O mortal, what is good;
and what does the Lord require of you
but to do justice, and to love kindness,
and to walk humbly with your God?" (v. 8)

Wesleyan spirituality insists on making a connection between our contemplation and our practice, between what we believe and what we do. This text from Micah makes the "doing" clear. How does it connect with the larger movement of God's grace?

The birth of Jesus isn't just the birth of one tiny human a long time ago, it's the birth of new life for the whole world, the birth of a new way of life for every human. The newness isn't because God hadn't been in the world before or because God's love, justice, or vision for the world changed. The birth of Jesus is new life for the whole world because in Jesus God reveals what it looks like to perfectly *do justice, love kindness, and walk humbly with God.* God is doing a new thing in Jesus—not just speaking through prophets or signs or dreams, but entering space and time, taking on all the lament and limitation of human life—to show us how to live and to love. In Jesus, God both reveals and empowers our capacity to grow into the truly human image God has always intended.

Whether you, like me, struggle to discern the perfect gift for loved ones, the good news for us all is that we know what God desires. God wants us to make room in our daily lives and decisions for the justice of Jesus to be born anew that we might sojourn in solidarity with those who are poor, vulnerable, marginalized, and victimized. God wants our hearts to receive and beat with the love and kindness of the Christ child that we might reach out in compassion and care for those longing for tenderness. God wants the humility of Jesus to live in our minds and spirits, tempering our tendency to think we have to get everything right or that we can accomplish things on our own. God's "wish list" is for us to make Christ's presence an enfleshed presence. Justice. Love and kindness. Humility. Those gifts are good for us and for all. They bear new life into the world. Every time.

Rev. Ginger E. Gaines-Cirelli

DECEMBER 29

Then he said to them, "These are my words that I spoke to you while I was still with you—that everything written about me in the law of Moses, the prophets, and the psalms must be fulfilled." Then he opened their minds to understand the scriptures, and he said to them, "Thus it is written, that the Messiah is to suffer and to rise from the dead on the third day, and that repentance and forgiveness of sins is to be proclaimed in his name to all nations, beginning from Jerusalem. You are witnesses of these things. And see, I am sending upon you what my Father promised; so stay here in the city until you have been clothed with power from on high."

Luke 24:44-49

I've often said, and I am certainly not the only one who has, that "God the Father sends God the Son. God the Son sends God the Spirit. God the Spirit sends the apostles (and all future believers, the church) into the world to be the primary agency to restore the world." In this short yet powerful phrase, one can understand the whole story line of the Bible—God is a missionary God, who longs for the world to be restored toward its intended wholeness, and God's people are the primary means in which God restores.

The purposeful sending activity of God is found throughout all of Scripture. It couldn't be more illumined, however, than in what we have come to know and refer to as the commissioning passages—

Matthew 28:18-20; Mark 16:15-18; John 20:21-23; Acts 1:8; and our reading for today, Luke 24:44-49. Each of these passages presents a different or unique perspective on the apostles' role as sent ones. However, when understood within the greater context of the entire gospel message, which is that in Jesus Christ there is salvation and justice, regardless of the unique perspective each passage presents, the purpose is clear—Christ-followers, whether eyewitnesses like those listening to Jesus's words in Luke 24:44-49, or modern-day, living examples, are to bear witness to the person and work of Jesus.

When I was a child, Christmas was about one thing, as it is for many—receiving gifts. When I was a teenager, Christmas was about two things—receiving gifts and a much-needed break from the repetitiveness of a high school education. As I've grown older, Christmas has become about something much bigger—a bigger narrative found within the season of Advent, a time in which we await the coming of Christ and remember the longing of the Jews for the Messiah, a Savior. This remembrance of the Jews waiting for liberation evokes our own personal and communal yearning for and need of forgiveness and salvation. This remembrance prompts us to look back to celebrate the birth of King Jesus *and* to look forward to a time when all things will be made new, or whole. The much-celebrated Advent themes of hope, peace, joy, and love remind us that Advent is also about bearing witness to God's work in the world as sent ones on a mission to restore the world toward its intended wholeness.

According to today's scripture passage, to be a faithful witness is to give evidence of "a change of heart and life for the forgiveness of sins, to all nations" (v. 47 CEB). Why? Because we are witnesses of the death, burial, and resurrection of Jesus, or as it says in verse 46,

"The Messiah is to suffer and to rise from the dead on the third day," and later, in verse 48, "You are witnesses of these things."

When we live on mission, we live seeking to observe and conform to the commission as sent ones, and we do so with what some might consider the greatest gift of all—heavenly power (v. 49). This heavenly power, the Holy Spirit, is our primary source of strength, courage, and resolve in which to bear witness to God's redeeming work. This Advent and Christmas season, welcome the greatest gift of all, the Spirit, into your life, and have the bravery to bear witness to the person and work of Christ where you live, work, study, or play. Bring hope, peace, joy, and love into a world that so eagerly awaits it and so desperately needs it.

Chris Folmsbee

DECEMBER 30

Jesus said to them again, "Peace be with you. As the Father has sent me, so I send you."

John 20:21

As a child, I looked forward to Christmas morning with excitement and expectation. My parents encouraged us to make lists of gifts we wanted, and Saturday morning commercials provided ample fuel as my Christmas list grew long. Then on Christmas morning, we opened the presents tucked under the tree as I held my breath, hoping my personal wish list would be fulfilled.

As the disciples followed Jesus, they looked forward with excitement and expectation to what the Messiah would accomplish. The disciples expected a warrior-king, who would rule with force and give them places of privilege. The events of Holy Week left the disciples holding their breath as their hopes seemed to end at the cross.

On Easter evening, the risen Christ appears to the disciples. Earlier, the disciples had found the unwrapped burial linens in the tomb, yet they locked themselves up in a room, trapped in fear. Instead of the harsh judgment the disciples deserve for denying Jesus, Christ gives them grace-filled blessing: "Peace be with you." Jesus offers this blessing of peace, not just once but repeatedly, and then breathes out the gift of the Holy Spirit on the disciples. The disciples are filled with joy. They breathe in the blessings of peace, unwrap themselves from their anxiety, and are sent by Jesus to share God's love in the world.

The blessing of peace in Jesus is not a one-time event. The gift of God in Jesus Christ, wrapped in swaddling clothes on Christmas morning and fully revealed on Easter evening, is a gift we are to share with the world repeatedly. Sharing the peace of Christ with neighbors and strangers is as fundamental to our spiritual lives as breathing is to our physical lives. The breath of Christ fills our lives with the Holy Spirit, and we are called to breathe out everyday blessings of peace to those around us.

Even though I've forgotten many of the gifts I desperately wanted as a child, I remember the love and joy I experienced on those Christmas mornings. That joy is available to each one of us every day in the peace of Christ. We are called to unwrap the love of God in our lives and freely share this gift with the entire world.

Rev. Todd Salmi

"But you will receive power when the Holy Spirit has come upon you; and you will be my witnesses in Jerusalem, in all Judea and Samaria, and to the ends of the earth."

Acts 1:8

I belong to a group of leaders who are on a "treasure hunt." We call ourselves the Church Pirates because we are out there searching for a treasure that we know God has hidden in plain sight. This treasure is the "power of the Holy Spirit," and we believe that it is already at work in Jerusalem, Judea, Samaria, and the ends of the earth. Our challenge is that as church leaders, we can't always see what's right in front of us, especially when it comes to all the good that God is doing in the world. So, our group is intentionally seeking this treasure that God has offered the world.

Ms. Georgia Calhoun is one of those treasures that we have met on our treasure hunt. She is an unassuming, beautiful woman with the most gentle voice. She met us at the national park in Anniston, Alabama, to teach us about the Freedom Riders. She is a retired schoolteacher who is passionate about ensuring that the story of the brave souls who worked toward integration is remembered and told. She proudly stood before us, showing the painting of the buses on the sides of the building, memorializing what had been done to the bus riders who were testing the new laws of intercoastal integration. A mob had threatened their lives by slashing the bus tires and throwing a homemade bomb in the broken windows of the bus while the passengers were still in their seats. Fifty years later, Ms. Georgia said, "Things have changed, but there are moments that are still difficult." When asked what will help us change, she said "Education is the key. We have got to teach our children and all people about loving our differences and not being afraid." That is the treasure we were seeking as she gave us a glimpse of the power of the Holy Spirit within her.

I marveled at the brave souls who were willing to put their lives at risk in order for all people to experience good in their lives and in the world. When Christ invited us to go and be his witnesses, it was not to go just to Jerusalem, or just to Samaria; it was to go to the ends of the earth. This means that Christians need to work together to ensure that we are doing, as John Wesley would urge, all the good we can, in all the places we can, so that all the people we encounter can experience God's goodness and grace. Like those Freedom Riders, we may encounter mobs who are against us, but when we have the power of the Holy Spirit on our side, we can endure and persevere. May God be with us as we do "all the good"!

Rev. Dr. Amy Valdez Barker